QUICK FIX SCIENCE

FORCES
AND
MAGNETS

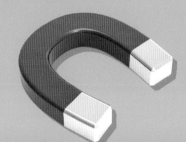

PAUL MASON

WAYLAND

First published in Great Britain in 2021
by Wayland
Copyright © Hodder and Stoughton, 2021
All rights reserved

Design: www.rocketdesign-ltd.co.uk
Editor: Nicola Edwards

HB ISBN: 978 1 5263 1587 8
PB ISBN: 978 1 5263 1588 5

Printed and bound in China

Wayland, an imprint of
Hachette Children's Group
Part of Hodder and Stoughton
Carmelite House
50 Victoria Embankment
London EC4Y 0DZ
An Hachette UK Company
www.hachette.co.uk
www.hachettechildrens.co.uk

MIX
Paper from
responsible sources
FSC
www.fsc.org
FSC® C104740

Cover and interior Snappy artwork by John Haslam

Picture acknowledgements:
Shutterstock: Africa Studio 16cl; Anamuka 29c; Avicon 16c; Aisyah Az Zahra 8-9b; Alex Bard 15cl; Bmszealand 10c; Cy Bo fr cover br, 20bl; Aleksey Boyko 19br; Alexey Broslavets 22tr; Marti Bug Catcher 7b; Marcel Clemens 5tl; Harry Collins Photography 17br; Max Dallocco, elements furnished by NASA 6-7tc, 8bl; Dvande 20br; Dwinsssdy 16tr; Svetlana Foote 27; Four Oaks 6br; grey_and 21cl; Jan Willem van Hofwegen 13tl, 13tr; Hope05 5bl; IvanC7 1, 21b; Akkjarat Jarusilawong 15br; J10 8-9c; Jumi Story 12t; Vladimir Korostyshevskiy 5c; Katerina Krasikova 13bl; Lightitup 24bc; Martine Liu 58 15tr; Lzf 19cr; Masik0553 13bc; Master1305 5tr; Matsabe 8-9c; Milagli 26cr; Milan1983 12b; Captain Milos 15cr; Mipan 3tl, 29t; Dina Morozova 11c; Nerthuz 8br, 9br; Nicku 9t; New Africa 5cr; Nicescene 23tr; Zoran Orcik 5cl; Maryna Osadcha 11t; Chalermpon Poungpeth 13cr; Pozitivo 16b; Quality Stock Arts 22br; Rawf8 22cr; Red Tiger 15bl; Revers f cover tl; Vladimir Rubanov 4b, 10b; Roman Samborskyi 17bl; Slowmotiongli 17bc; snapgalleria 25t; Ody Stocker 22bl; stockyimages 6bc; Suit Stock Photo 23tl; Sunward Art 3tr, 21cr; Taffpixture 7c; Tartila 10cr; Vibrant Image Studio 6cl; Vvoe 26bl; Wasantha 8958 18t; Wavebreakmedia 4c; White vector 17t; Suwat wongkham f cover cr; Carlos Yudica f cover tr; Yuriy2012 18-19c; Zizou7 25b.

Every attempt has been made to clear copyright. Should there be any inadvertent omission, please apply to the publisher for rectification.

Meet Snappy.

Snappy is a young
Nile crocodile.

Most crocodiles are only
interested in eating and
sleeping, but Snappy
is different.

Snappy is interested in
science, too.

CONTENTS

WHAT ARE FORCES?

Forces are pushes and pulls. Look around and you will see that we use them all the time.

To keep hold of something that wants to get away, we use pulling force:

Must ... hold ... on.

Mustn't ... fall ... over.

← Pull!

Pull! →

See if you can work out some of the forces in these photos (warning: one of them is a joke). Think about air resistance, friction, gravity and magnetism.

Find out if you were right on page 31.

1. Which force keeps this rock climber's shoes sticking to the rock face?

To pedal a bicycle or get speed on a skateboard, we use a pushing force:

Push! Push!

To cut a slice of bread, people push AND pull on the knife.

Push!

Pull!

2. Which force causes a skydiver to fall? And which force slows them down?

3. How does this street performer float in the air?

4. Which force keeps these things stuck to the fridge door?

GRAVITY

This first force is one that's useful for everyone – including crocodiles who want to stay in their river …

This force is called gravity. It is a pulling force. Here are three top gravity facts:

Gravity

In real life there would not be a label on this scene to show you gravity. Gravity would be invisible.

1.

Gravity is invisible

You cannot see gravity. You can only see its effects.

2.

Everything has gravity

All objects have gravity – from lightweight insects to tiny pebbles and whole **planets**.

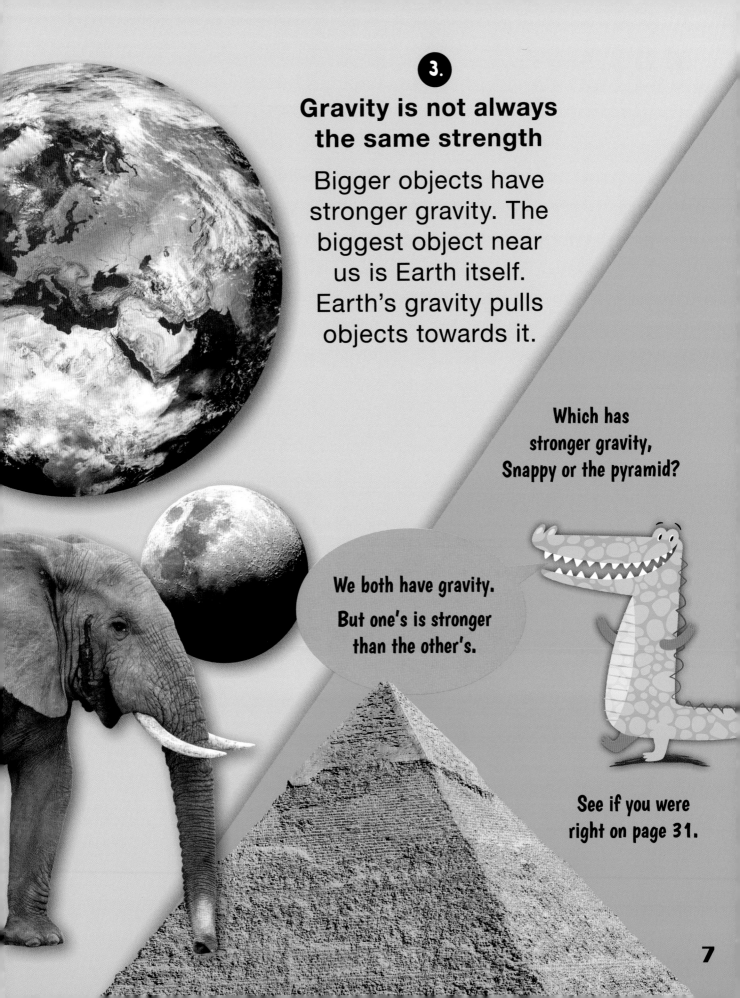

3.

Gravity is not always the same strength

Bigger objects have stronger gravity. The biggest object near us is Earth itself. Earth's gravity pulls objects towards it.

Which has stronger gravity, Snappy or the pyramid?

We both have gravity.

But one's is stronger than the other's.

See if you were right on page 31.

WEIGHT

Some objects are harder to pick up than others, because they weigh more. A heavy fish is a good thing, of course! Yum!

Weight is a force caused by gravity's pull. Gravity is stronger on big planets than small ones. This means a person's weight would be different on some planets than others:

If you weighed 40 kg on Earth (or roughly five dachshunds),

... on Mars, you would weigh 15 kg (as much as two dachshunds),

Mars' gravity = 37.2 of Earth's gravity

Newtons

Like all forces, weight can be measured in Newtons. Newtons are named after Sir Isaac Newton, the scientist who first described gravity and how it works.

Hair: 0/10
Science genius-ing: 10/10

... on Neptune you would weigh 46 kg (or roughly six dachshunds),

... on Jupiter you would weigh 101 kg (which is 13.5 dachshunds).

Neptune's gravity = 114% of Earth's gravity

Jupiter's gravity = 253.1% of Earth's gravity

FRICTION

Friction is a pulling force. It happens when one object rubs against another – like when you slide down a dry riverbank.

Whenever an object rubs against something, it produces friction. Rubbing together with bigger force produces more friction.

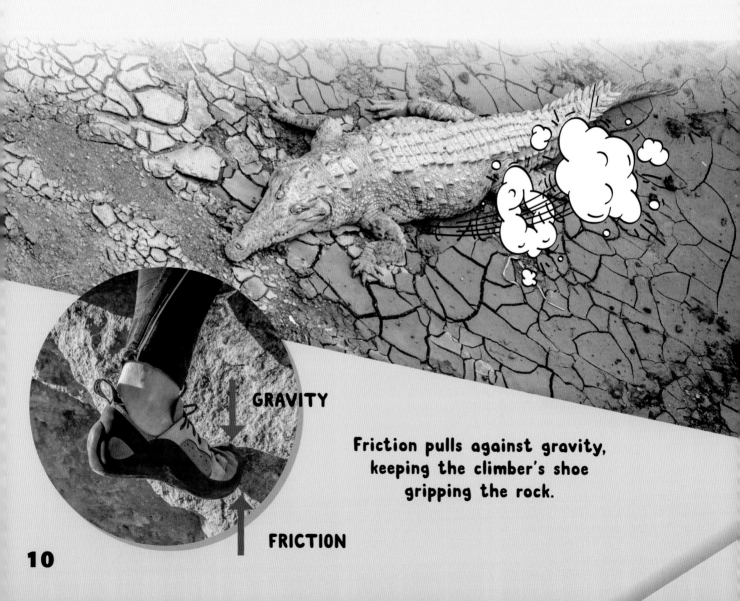

GRAVITY

FRICTION

Friction pulls against gravity, keeping the climber's shoe gripping the rock.

Rough v. smooth

Whenever two objects move against each other, they produce friction. If one or both of them has a rough surface – like sandpaper, for example – they produce more friction.

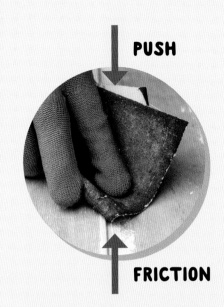

Using rough sandpaper means you have to push with a lot of force.

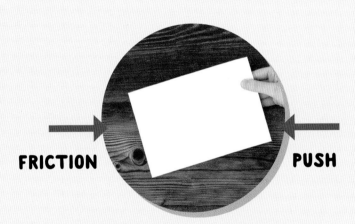

Pushing ordinary paper across wood needs less force.

Which would make more friction between the climbing shoe and the rock?

a) a climber weighing 70 kg

b) a climber weighing 40 kg

c) both make the same friction

See if you're right on page 31.

FRICTION IS HOT STUFF

Friction can be a pain – literally. Friction produces heat ... sometimes enough heat to burn you.

Friction yourself

Try rubbing your hands lightly together.

Now do the same, but pressing them together hard.

Do they feel warmer one way than the other?

Friction can be useful if you want to start a fire, or grip on to a surface (like the climber on page 10).

FORCE

MOVEMENT

FRICTION

HEAT

Fighting friction

One way to fight friction is to push against it with a bigger force:

1 x crocodile = less force

Amount of friction is the same.

2 x crocodiles = more force

You can also fight friction by adding a slippery layer between the two objects. Can you spot how friction is being defeated in these photos?

 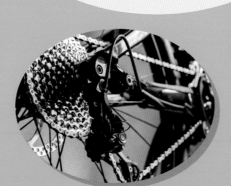

Find out if you were right on page 31.

WATER RESISTANCE

Water resistance is a pulling force. It is the pull of water on objects that are trying to move through it.

Snappy is catching the frightened human because of water resistance. Small objects feel less water resistance than big ones.

AAAAARGH!

I just want to be friends!

Small outline
= less water
resistance
= faster

Big outline
= more water
resistance
= slower

Check your water resistance

Next time you go swimming, do a push-off from the side of the pool with your arms sticking out from your sides.

After that, push off with your arms stretched out ahead of you, in a more arrow-like shape.

Which gets you further?

Which of these do you think feels least water resistance? Find out on page 31.

A

kingfisher

B

bomber

C

elephant going for a swim

15

AIR RESISTANCE

Humans don't move very fast in the water, but they CAN run away quickly on land.

On land, water resistance does not slow you down. Another force, called air resistance, DOES slow you down – but not as much.

Shape

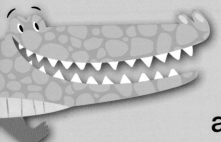

Imagine trying to cut your food with a wrong-way-up knife. It would be much harder than normal. In the same way, an object's shape affects how much air resistance it feels.

The supercar feels less air resistance.

Air flow

Air flows smoothly around the pointy shape of this supercar.

Air flow

Air hits the flat front of the truck and cannot flow smoothly.

The truck feels more air resistance.

Put these living things in order of which would meet LEAST air resistance. Find out if you were right on page 31.

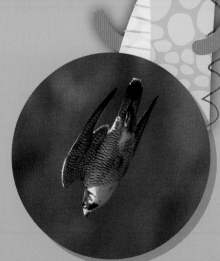

PULLEYS, LEVERS AND GEARS

Have you ever seen a leopard dragging an antelope up a tree? It looks like very hard work! I wonder if it could be made easier ...

So heavy!

Imagine trying to pull an injured climber up a cliff (which is a BIT like pulling an antelope up a tree).

Gnnnnnn!

rescuer

50 kg

Pulling them straight up would be impossible:

Help!

50 kg

injured climber

There is a way to rescue the climber, though – use a simple pulley:

Pulleys are not the only way to increase force. Here are two other useful ones:

Phew!

Half held by tree

25 kg

Half pulled by the rescuer

At last ...

50 kg

When you have to ride up a steep hill, gears make it much easier.

If you have to move something that does not want to move, a lever makes it easier.

MAGNETISM

Magnetism is a force that mystified people for thousands of years. (Crocodiles are WAY ahead of you. We've been using it for millions of years (see page 27).)

What is it that makes magnetism so mysterious? It's because magnetism is like other forces in some ways, but different in others:

1. Magnetism can be a push or a pull.

This train is held up by magnetism, which pushes it away from the ground.

These pieces of scrap metal are being lifted by magnetism, which is pulling them upwards.

2. Like gravity, magnetism affects objects it does not touch.

Unlike gravity, though, magnetism does not affect ALL objects.

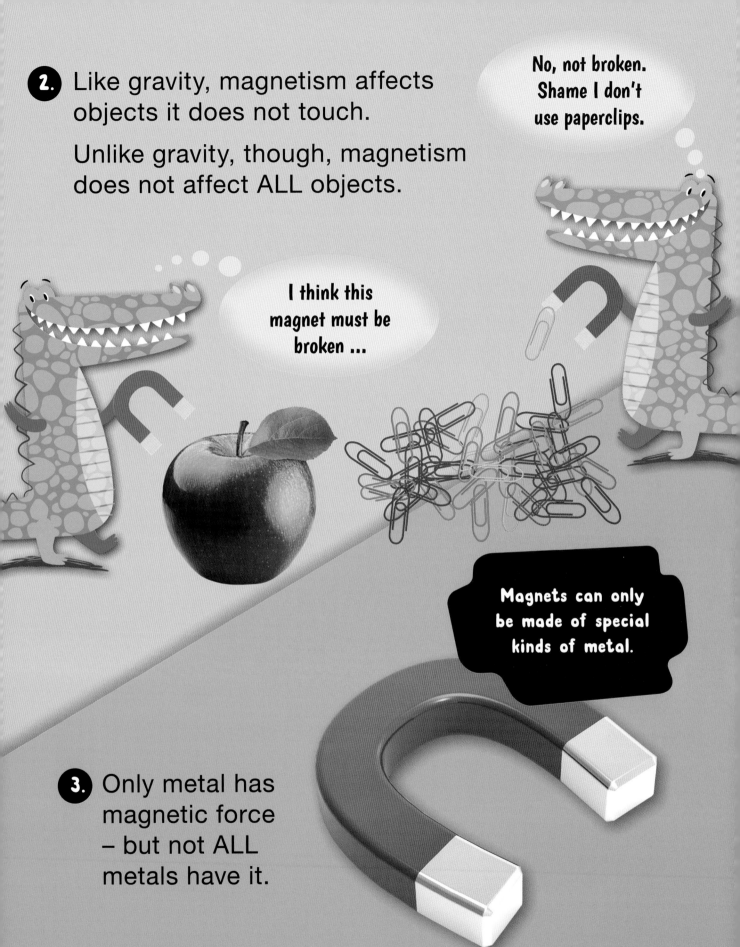

3. Only metal has magnetic force – but not ALL metals have it.

MAGNETIC ATTRACTION

I really can't work out magnetism! My Egypt souvenir magnet just WON'T stick to any of the trees or rocks where I live.

Magnetism test

To help Snappy work out magnetism, you need a magnet, a piece of paper and a pencil. Walk around seeing what the magnet will stick to. You could start with these, but try to test at least 12 different objects. Here are a few ideas to start you off.

Fridge

Brick wall

Car door

Toy dinosaur

Window

Draw out a table like this one and make a note of where each object fits:

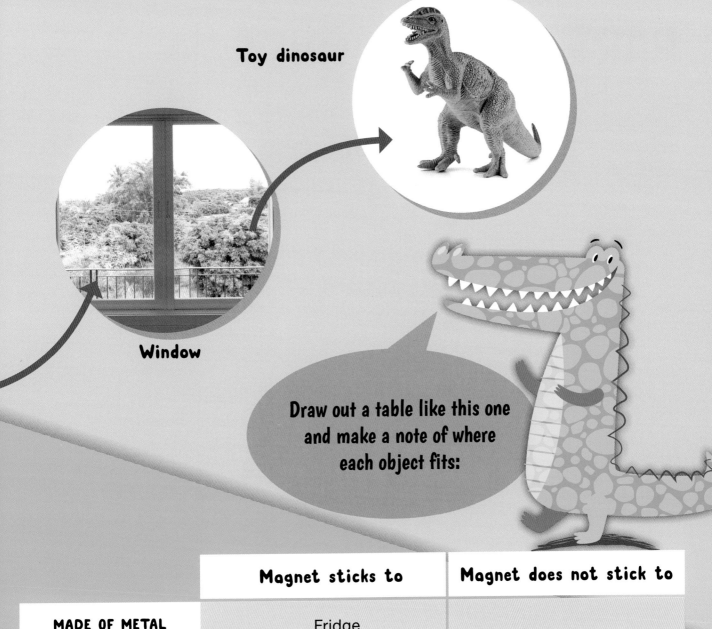

	Magnet sticks to	Magnet does not stick to
MADE OF METAL	Fridge	
NOT MADE OF METAL		Brick wall

The answers will give you some clues about what kind of material feels the force of magnetism. The table will tell you:

1. Are all the 'sticks to' objects made of metal?
2. Are all the metal objects also 'sticks to'?

Check if your table was right on page 31.

PARTS OF A MAGNET

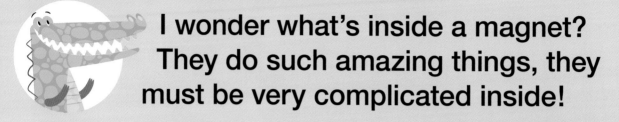

I wonder what's inside a magnet? They do such amazing things, they must be very complicated inside!

In fact, magnets do not have complicated parts. They ARE different inside, though.

NON-MAGNET
Little force fields (called 'domains') point in different directions.

MAGNET
Domains point in same direction

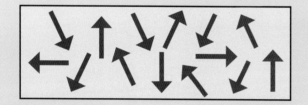

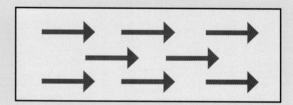

The lined-up domains are like this dog team, all pulling in the same direction. They are what give a magnet its force.

Poles: pulling and pushing

Magnets have two ends, called the north pole and the south pole. The poles affect how magnets behave toward each other:

• if different poles point at each other, the magnets pull together or attract

• if the same poles point at each other, the magnets push away or repel.

A magnet's force becomes weaker as it gets further away.

Magnetic field

Will these magnets
a) pull towards each other or
b) push apart?

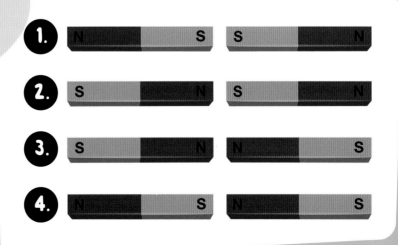

1. N   S   S   N
2. S   N   S   N
3. S   N   N   S
4. N   S   N   S

The answers are on page 31.

MAGNET EARTH

You've probably heard of the North and South Poles (freezing cold places that no self-respecting crocodile would ever visit). Yes – the same names as the ends of a magnet!

Earth itself is a giant magnet. At its core is lots of hot metal that is magnetic. It makes a giant version of the magnetic field on page 25.

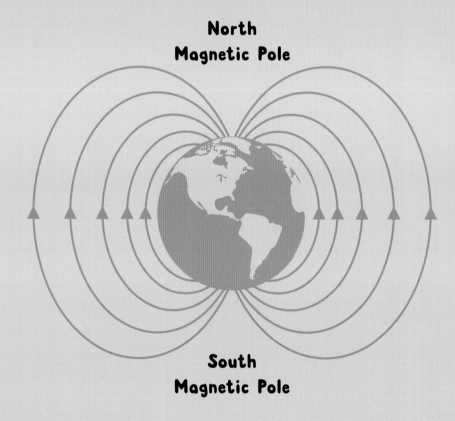

North Magnetic Pole

South Magnetic Pole

Centuries ago, travellers used magnetic stones to help find their direction. The stones were affected by Earth's magnetism and pointed north-south.

Animal magnetism

Scientists think that many animals – including birds, fish, insects and crocodiles – use Earth's magnetic field to navigate.

When humans in Florida, USA, want a crocodile to stop living nearby, they:

1. Catch it.

2. Tape magnets to the sides of its head.

3. Take the crocodile away.

The magnets stop me knowing which way is home.

4. Remove the magnets before letting it go.

MAGNETS ALL AROUND US

Horseshoes, rings, buttons and bars ... No, they are not unusual objects found in vacuum-cleaner bags! They are different kinds of magnet.

Bar magnets and horseshoe magnets

A magnet is most powerful at its poles. Because bar magnets have narrow poles, they are not very strong.

Horseshoe magnets are bar magnets bent into a horseshoe shape. Because both poles point the same way, these magnets are stronger.

Bar magnet

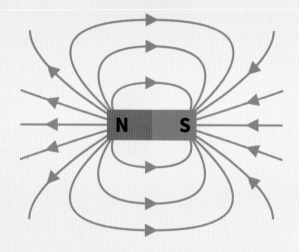

N S

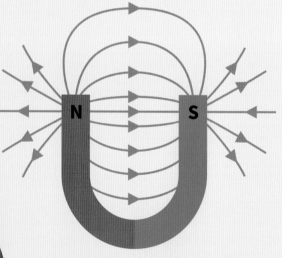

N S

Horseshoe magnet

Horseshoe magnets are a symbol for magnetism all around the world.

Button magnets

The flat ends of button magnets give them a large pole for their size. This makes button magnets strong.

Huge button magnet

Button magnet

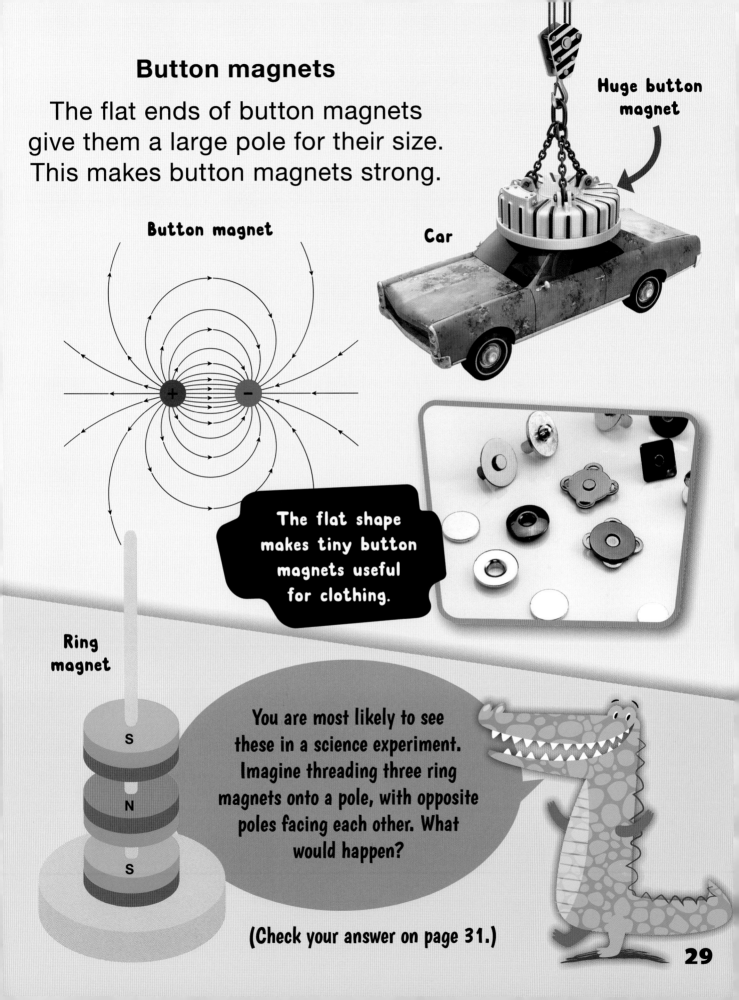

Car

The flat shape makes tiny button magnets useful for clothing.

Ring magnet

S

N

S

You are most likely to see these in a science experiment. Imagine threading three ring magnets onto a pole, with opposite poles facing each other. What would happen?

(Check your answer on page 31.)

GLOSSARY

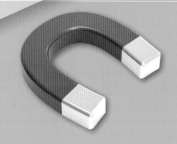

attract pull towards

core middle or centre of an object (often a round-shaped object)

domain tiny area inside an object that has a magnetic field

force field an area of energy surrounding an object. Magnets have a magnetic field

gears wheels or discs with teeth on the outside edge. Gears can be used to change the amount of force needed to move an object

lever solid bar resting on a pivot, which can be used to lift or move apart heavy objects

outline shape made by the outside edge of an object

planet large object in space that moves around a star. The Earth is a planet, moving around the Sun (which is a star)

pulley something (usually a small wheel with a groove around its edge) that changes the direction in which a rope or cable is travelling

repel push away

science study of how the physical world works

skydiver person so brave/ stupid that they are willing to jump out of an aeroplane and use a parachute to float to the ground

symbol shape that is used to represent something

ANSWERS

Page 5
1 Friction (page 10).
2 Gravity (see page 6) and air resistance (page 16).
3 He doesn't: it's a trick.
4 Magnetism (page 20).

Page 7
The pyramid is bigger than Snappy, so it has stronger gravity.

Page 10/11
a) The climber who weighs most will make the strongest friction. This is because weight is a force and objects that rub together with more force have more friction.

Page 13
The ice skate beats friction using a layer of unfrozen water; the bicycle chain uses oil; the water-park slide uses water.

Page 15
a) The kingfisher would feel least water resistance, because it is a) small and b) very pointy-shaped.

Page 17
1 Peregrine falcon (maximum speed over 300 kph); 2 cheetah (over 100 kph); 3 human (world record speed: 40+ kph).

Page 23
1 Yes, everything magnets stick to is made of metal.
2 Not necessarily, because magnets only stick to certain kinds of metal. Usually the metal contains iron, nickel or cobalt.

Page 25
1 S/S: repel
2 N/S: attract
3 N/N: repel
4 S/N: attract

Page 29
The magnets would repel each other, so they would hover without touching.

FINDING OUT MORE

Books to read

Science in a Flash! Forces, Georgia Amson-Bradshaw, (Franklin Watts, 2017)
This contains not only information about forces, starting with a flash headline then exploring further, but also some great jokes and cartoons.

Extreme Science: Powerful Forces, Jon Richards and Rob Colson (Wayland, 2019)
This book looks at forces in action, from the powerful pushes and pulls that create high speeds to the crushing forces that can change an object's shape or make it explode.

Be A Scientist: Investigating Forces, Jacqui Bailey (Wayland, 2019)
If you want to understand forces, don't only take our word for it – do some experiments of your own! This book will get you started as a Junior Science Expert.

Websites to visit

wowscience.co.uk
The sidebar tab for 'Forces and magnets' will lead to some fun experiments, which you could do in class or at home with an adult to help.

spaceplace.nasa.gov/what-is-gravity/en/
This web page for kids is about gravity. It is from the National Aeronautics and Space Administration (NASA) in the USA.

ducksters.com
Click on 'Science', then 'Physics', then look under the **Motion** heading to find more information about weight, force, gravity, friction and more. The website is quite serious, but a good place to find out information quickly.

INDEX